The Stations of the Cross

Introduction to
Zoe Cameron's Stations of the Cross

It is a great pleasure for me to write this introductory note to Zoe's imaginative and challenging engagement with the Stations of the Cross. Imaginative because she has obviously approached the subject with an artist's perspective, and not as someone coming from within an established conception about how the Stations should be depicted, and challenging because the imagery she conveys presents the Stations in a context that is not immediately familiar or safe; not for Zoe a typecast representation of first century Palestinian figures. Instead she has attempted, and to my mind succeeded, in making the Stations more universal, more timeless.

Her use of figures is particularly bold: we have Veronica as a typical housewife finding the cloth depicting Jesus's face, and holding it up as if asking if anyone had dropped it; we have the women of Jerusalem as three Eastern European (or so they seem to me) women in despair in a corn field; and, more disturbingly, the image of a stricken Jesus as the back-drop to two boys terrorising a third with guns, either in play or as a representative of urban gang culture is not known. This has the effect of universalising the Stations, making them cross-cultural with a vivid immediacy.

Then there are other artistic fingerprints that make these Stations universal in time as well as in place: whilst the dead Jesus is in his mother's arms, an ascending figure is being welcomed by an ancient God-like figure surrounded by angels in an almost direct reference to Renaissance depictions of heaven; whilst another image shows cherubs assisting with the Resurrection in a scene that could almost be by Lippi or his contemporaries. So fifteenth century angels share a canvas with 1960s housewives, and perfect sense it makes, too.

As separate works each has their own message to convey, but threaded together by the architecture of the All Saints Chapel they have a unity which makes their overall effect powerful and refreshing. In short Zoe makes us see something familiar with fresh eyes, and I, for one, am very grateful to her for her insight into the eternal mystery of the Passion of Jesus Christ.

Roger Bush, Dean of Truro.

Truro Cathedral

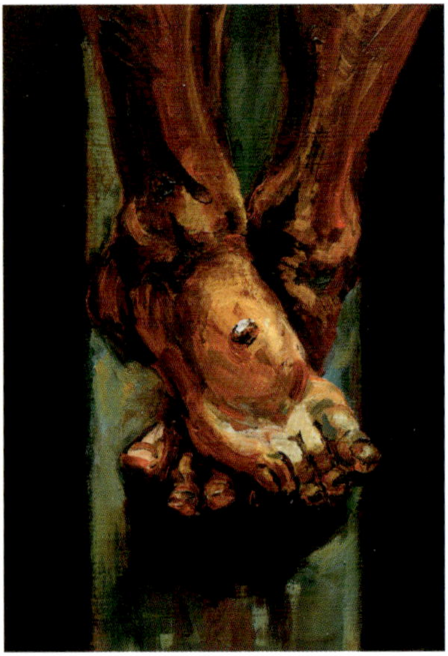

The Call

Come, my Way, my Truth, my Life:
Such a Way, as gives us breath:
Such a Truth, as ends all strife:
Such a Life, as killeth death.
Come, my Light, my Feast, my Strength:
Such a Light, as shows a feast:
Such a Feast, as mends in length:
Such a Strength, as makes his guest.
Come, my Joy, my Love, my Heart:
Such a Joy, as none can move:
Such a Love, as none can part:
Such a Heart, as joyes in love.

George Herbert

Jesus in the Garden of Gethsemane.

Luke 22 : 39 - 44. Jesus went out as usual to the Mount of Olives, and his disciples followed him. On reaching the place, he said to them, "Pray that you will not fall into temptation." He withdrew about a stones's throw beyond them, knelt down and prayed, "Father, if you are willing, take this cup from me; yet not my will, but yours be done."An Angel appeared to him and strengthened him. And being in anguish, he prayed more earnestly, and his sweat was like drops of blood falling to the ground.

I said to my soul, be still, and wait without hope
For hope would be hope for the wrong thing; wait without love
For love would be love of the wrong thing; there is yet faith
But the faith and the love and the hope are all in the waiting.
Wait without thought, for you are not ready for thought:
So the darkness shall be the light, and the stillness the dancing.

T.S. Eliot
(The Four Quartets)

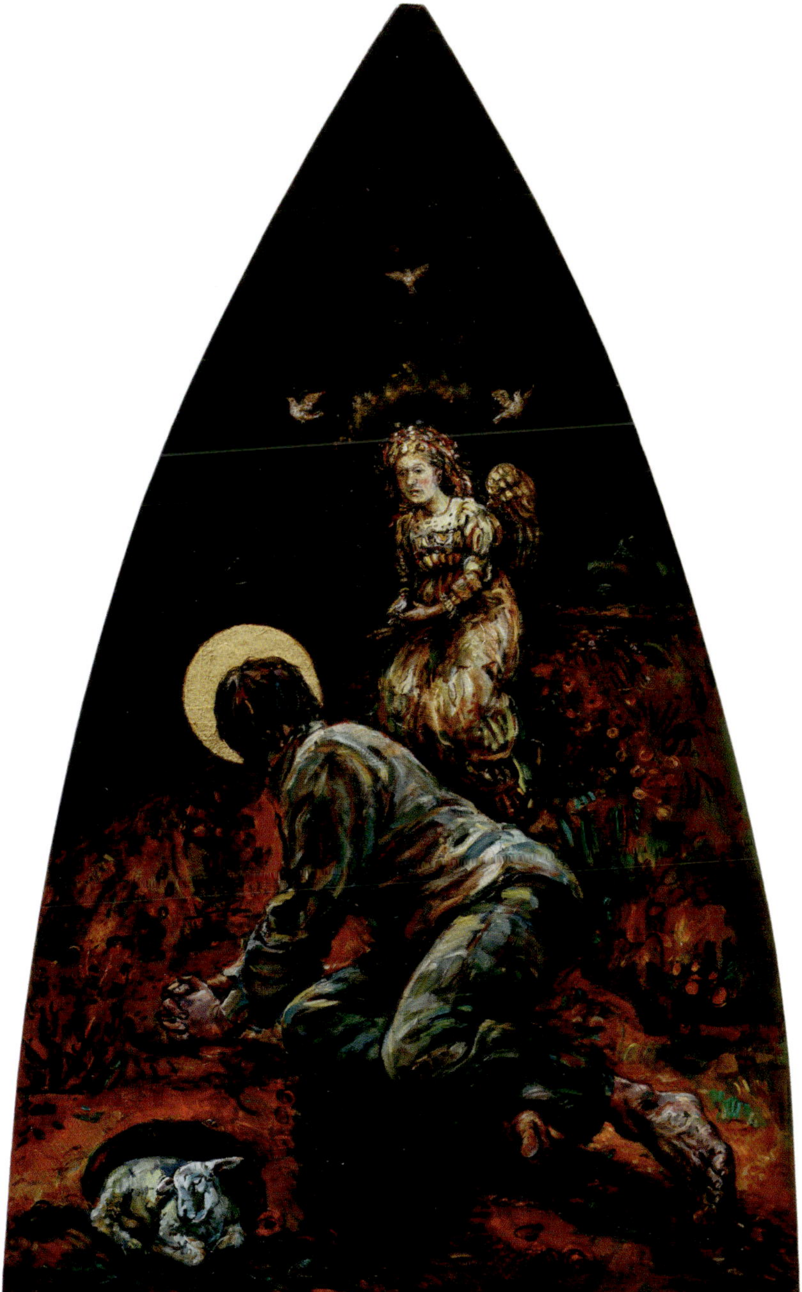

Jesus is Condemned.

Mark 15: 12 - 15."What shall I do then with the one you call king of the Jews ?" Pilate asked them. "Crucify him!" they shouted. "Why ? What crime has he committed?" asked Pilate. But they all shouted louder, "Crucify him!"
Wanting to satisfy the crowd, Pilate released Barabbas to them. He had Jesus flogged, and handed him over to be crucified.

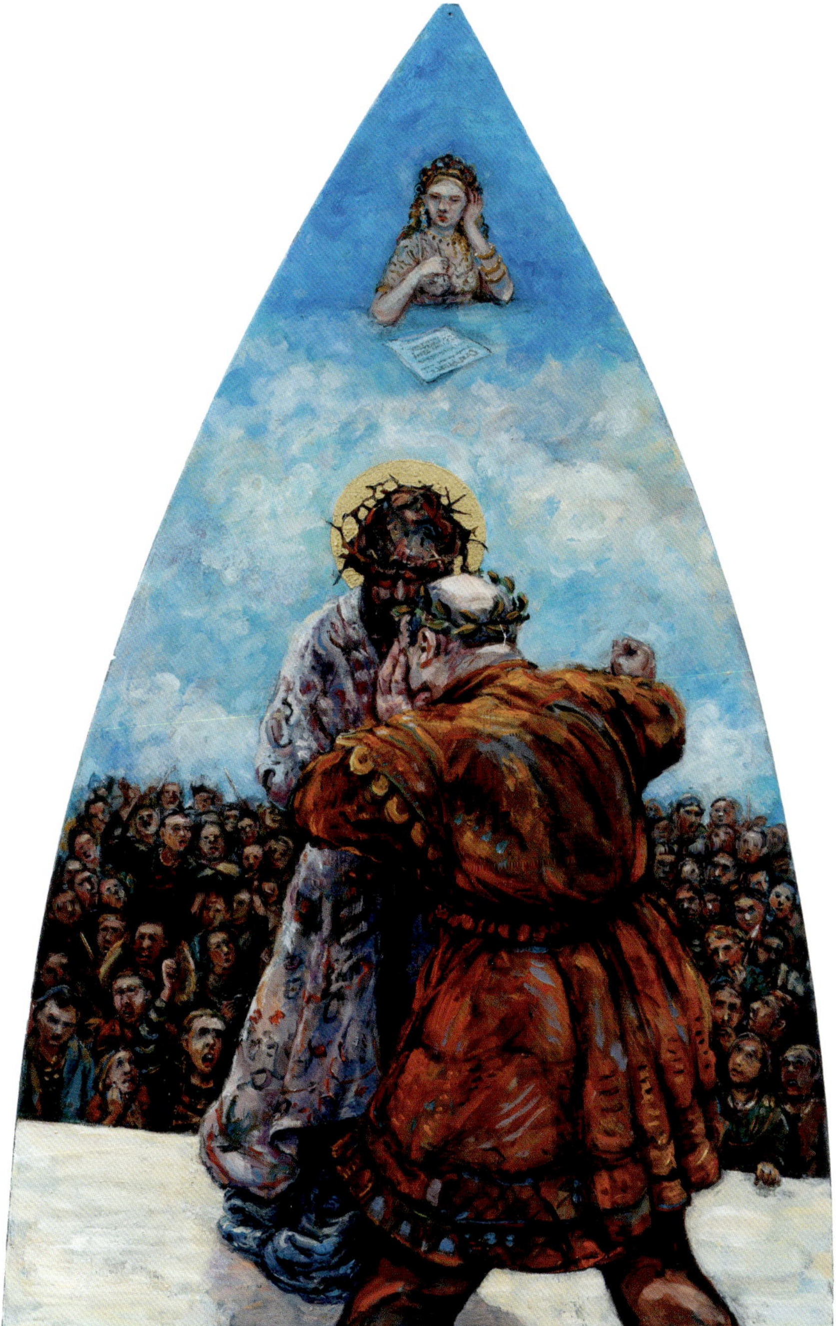

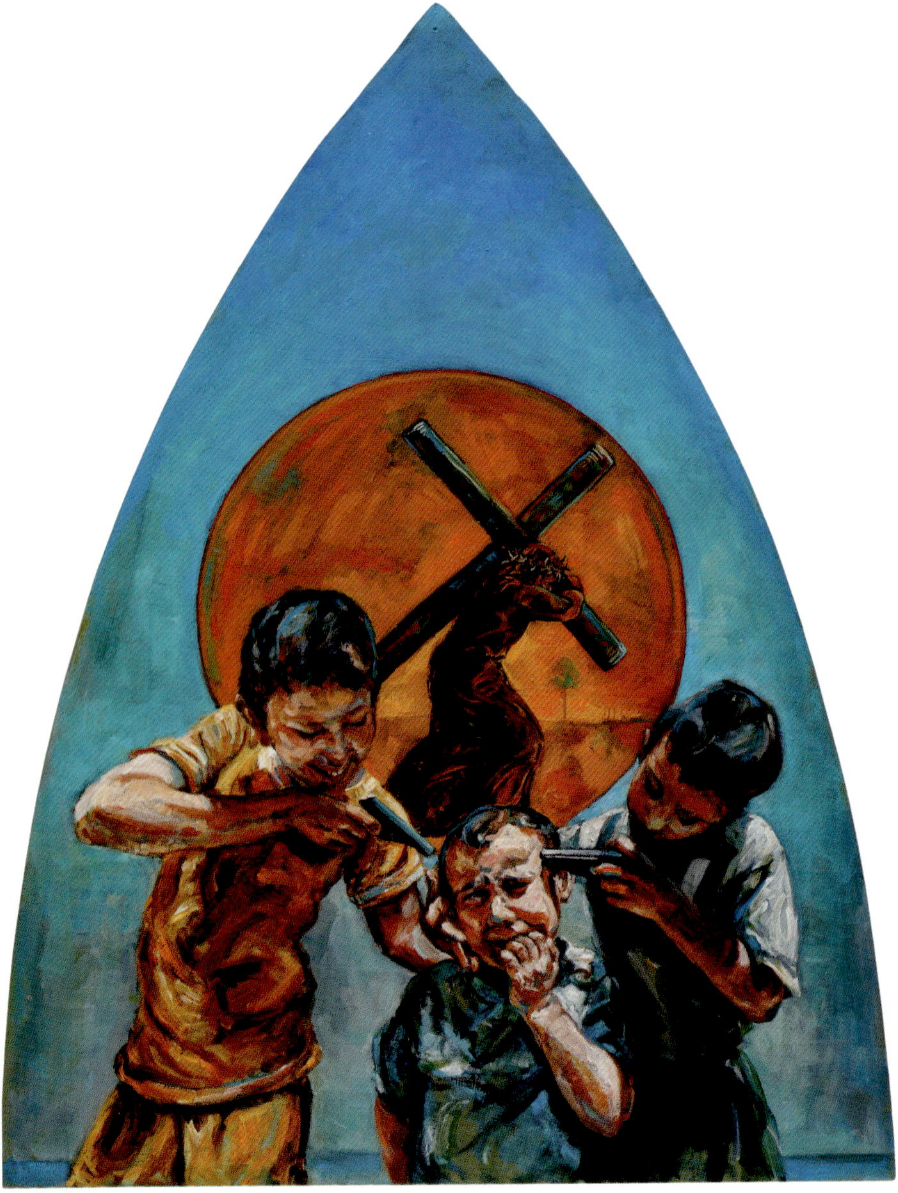

The Cross is laid upon him.

John 19 : 16 - 18. So the soldiers took charge of Jesus. Carrying his own cross, he went out to the place of the Skull (which in Aramaic is called Golgotha).

Madonna and Child.

The wings of the cherubim carry Him
whom the arms of Mary carried;
the God whom nothing can contain
did Mary contain and carry.
The King before whom the angels
of fire and spirit tremble
lies in the bosom of a girl,
and she cuddles Him as a baby.
The heaven is the throne for His glory,
Yet He sits on Mary's knees;
the earth too is His footstool,
Yet like a baby He crawls beside her.

St Ephraim of Syria

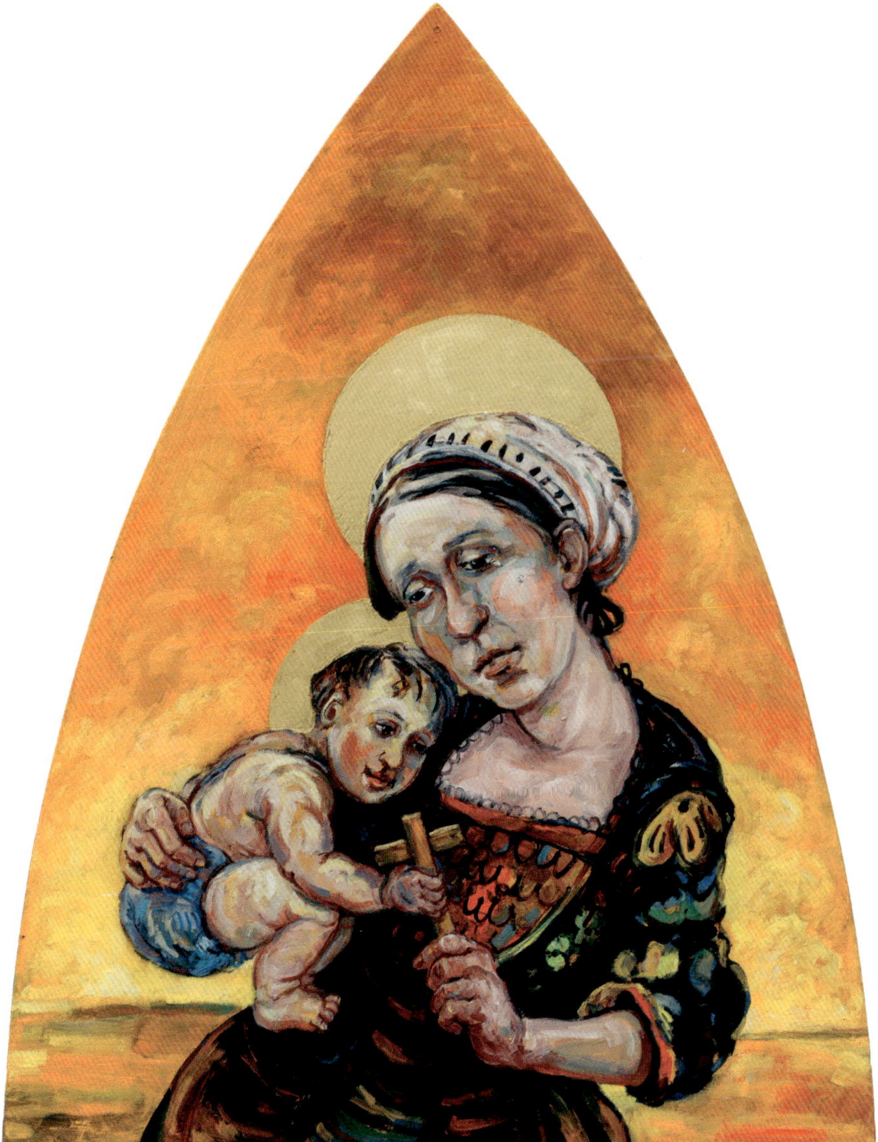

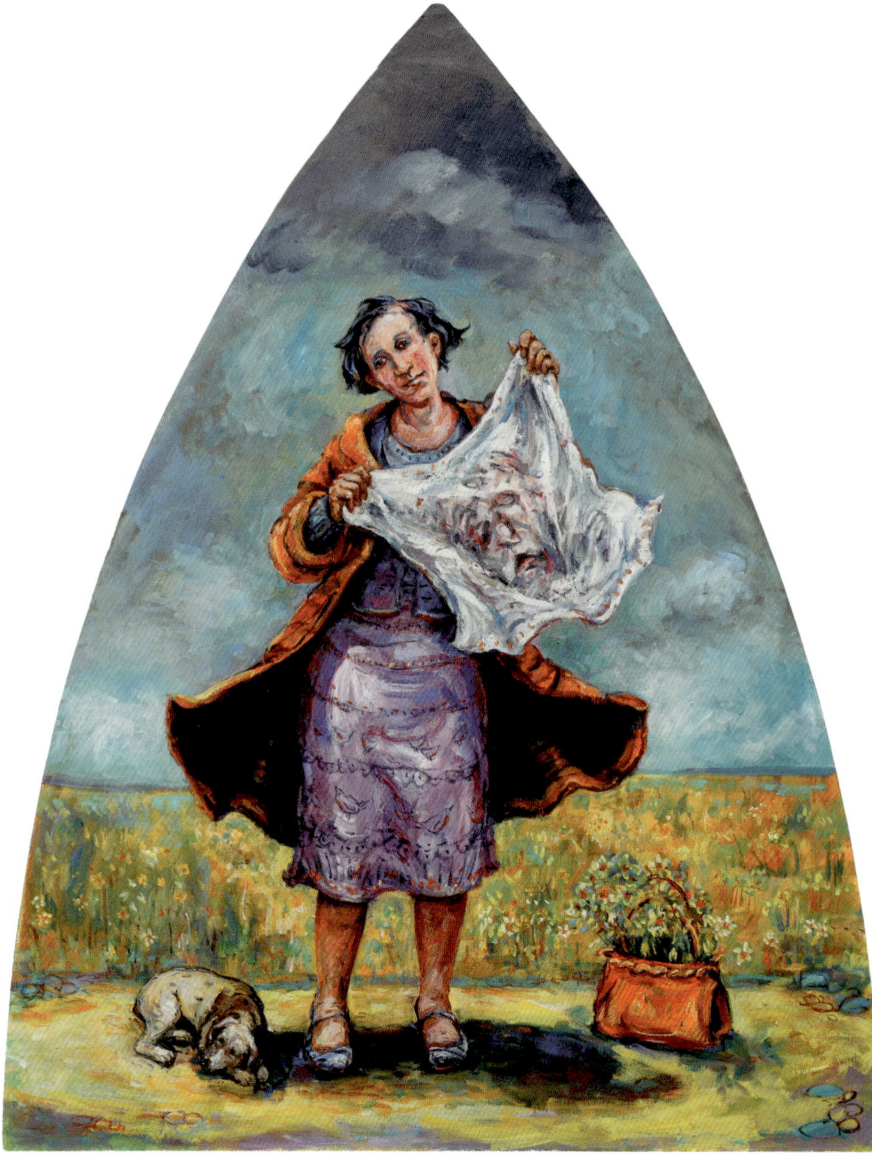

Veronica wipes the face of Jesus.

God's Grandeur

The world is charged with the grandeur of God,
It will flame out, like shining from shook foil;
It gathers to a greatness, like the ooze of oil
Crushed. Why do men then now not reck his rod?
Generations have trod, have trod, have trod;
And all is seared with trade; bleared, smeared with toil;
And wears man's smudge and shares man's smell: the soil
Is bare now, nor can foot feel, being shod.

And for all this, nature is never spent;
There lives the dearest freshness deep down things;
And though the last lights off the black West went
Oh, morning, at the brown brink eastward, springs
Because the Holy Ghost over the bent
World broods with warm breast and with ah! bright wings.

Gerard Manley Hopkins

Women weep.

Luke 23:27 - 31. A large number of people followed him, including women who mourned and wailed for him. Jesus turned and said to them, "Daughters of Jerusalem, do not weep for me; weep for yourselves and for your children. For the time will come when you will say, 'Blessed are the barren women, the wombs that never bore and the breasts that never nursed!' Then they will say to the mountains, 'Fall on us!' and to the hills 'Cover us!' " For if men do these things when the tree is green, what will happen when it is dry?"

When will you ever,
Peace, wild wooddove, shy wings shut,
Your round me roaming end, and under be my boughs?

Gerard Manley Hopkins

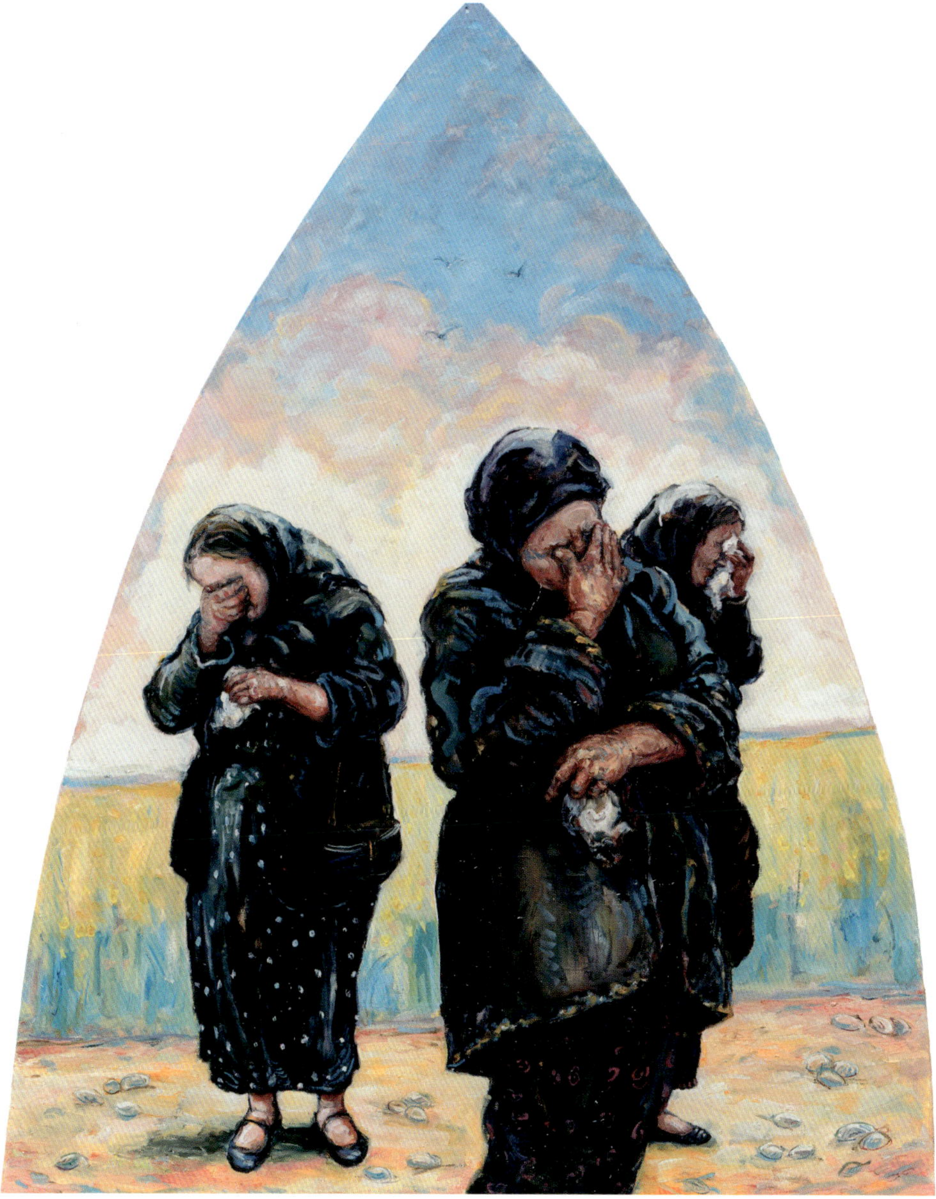

The Crucifixion.

Luke 23: 44 - 46. It was now about the sixth hour, and darkness came over the whole land until the ninth hour, for the sun stopped shining. And the curtain of the temple was torn in two. Jesus called out with a loud voice, "Father, into your hands I commit my spirit." When he had said this, he breathed his last.

I stretched out my hands and approached my Lord: For the stretching of my hands is His sign: My expansion is the outspread tree which was set up on the way of the Righteous One. And I became of no account to those who did not take hold of me; and I shall be with those who love me.

The Odes of Solomon, the Son of David.

Jesus is taken down from the Cross.

Isaiah 53 : 6 - 7. We all, like sheep, have gone astray,
each of us has turned to his own way;
and the Lord has laid upon him the iniquity of us all.
He was oppressed and afflicted, yet he did not open his mouth.
he was led like a lamb to the slaughter, and as a sheep before her shearers is silent, so he did not open his mouth.

In the crucified Christ forgiveness is offered and life is given. For humanity it is no longer a matter of fearing judgement or of meriting salvation, but of welcoming love and trust in humanity. For God has allowed himself to be murdered to offer his life even to the murderers.

Christ's death on the cross is a judgement of judgement.

Maximus The Confessor

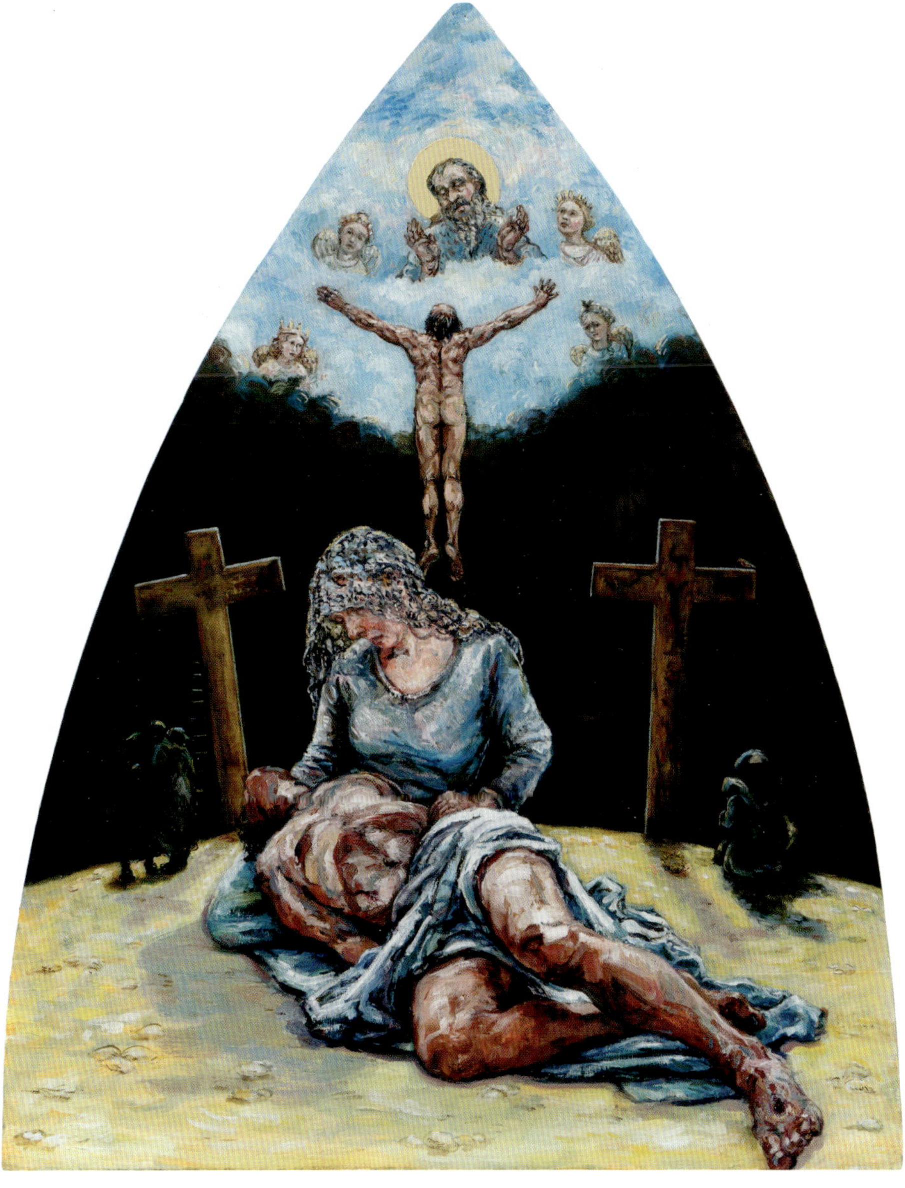

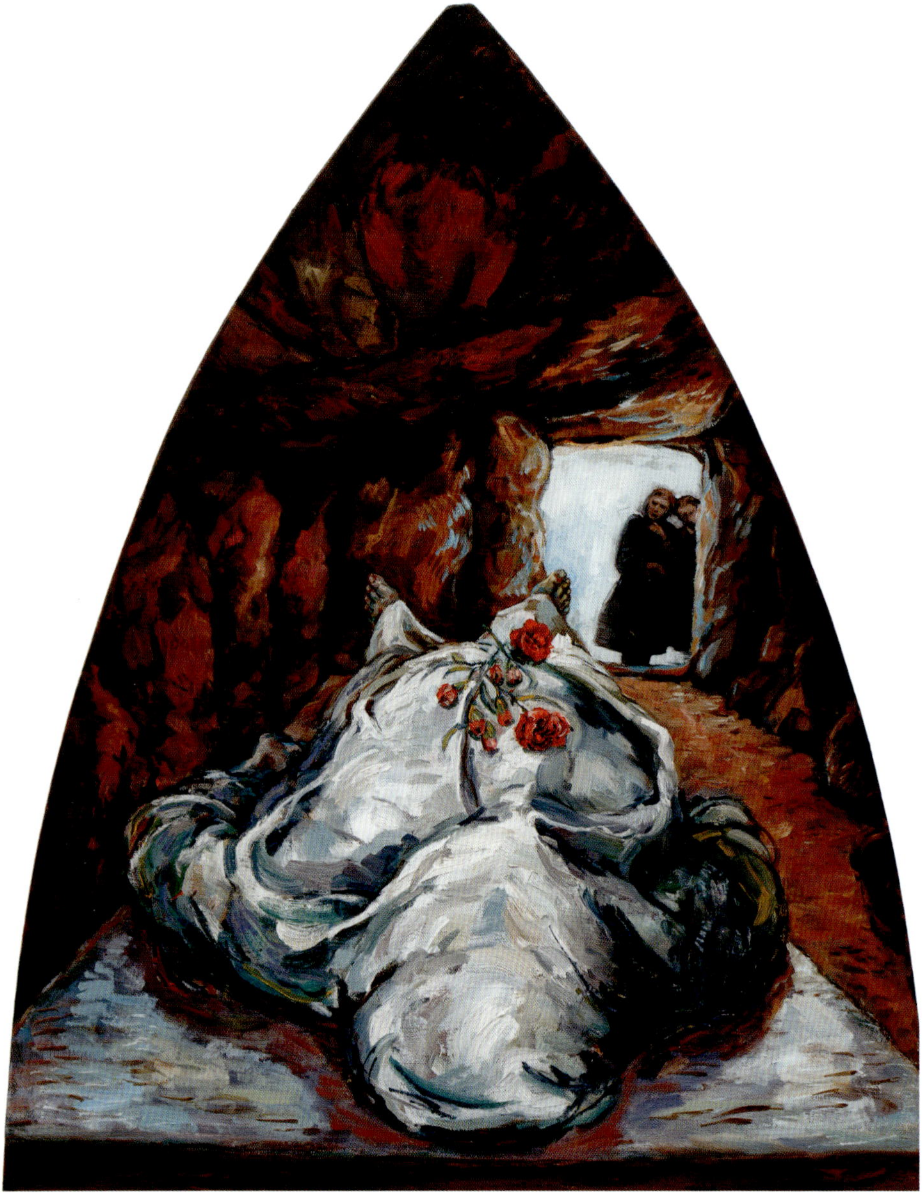

In the tomb.

Ephesians 3:18 - 19. And I pray that you, being rooted and established in love may have power, together with all the saints, to grasp how wide and long and high and deep is the love of Christ, and to know this love that surpasses knowledge - that you may be filled to the measure of all the fulness of God.

What is happening? Today there is a great silence over the earth, a great silence, and stillness, a great silence because the King sleeps.

An ancient homily.

The Resurrection.

Psalm 116 : 8 - 9. For you, O Lord, have delivered my soul from death, my eyes from tears, my feet from stumbling, that I may walk before the Lord in the land of the living.

Yesterday I was crucified with Christ; today I am glorified with him.

Yesterday I was dead with him; today I am sharing in his resurrection.

Yesterday I was buried with him; today I am waking with him from the sleep of death.

Gregory Nazianzen.

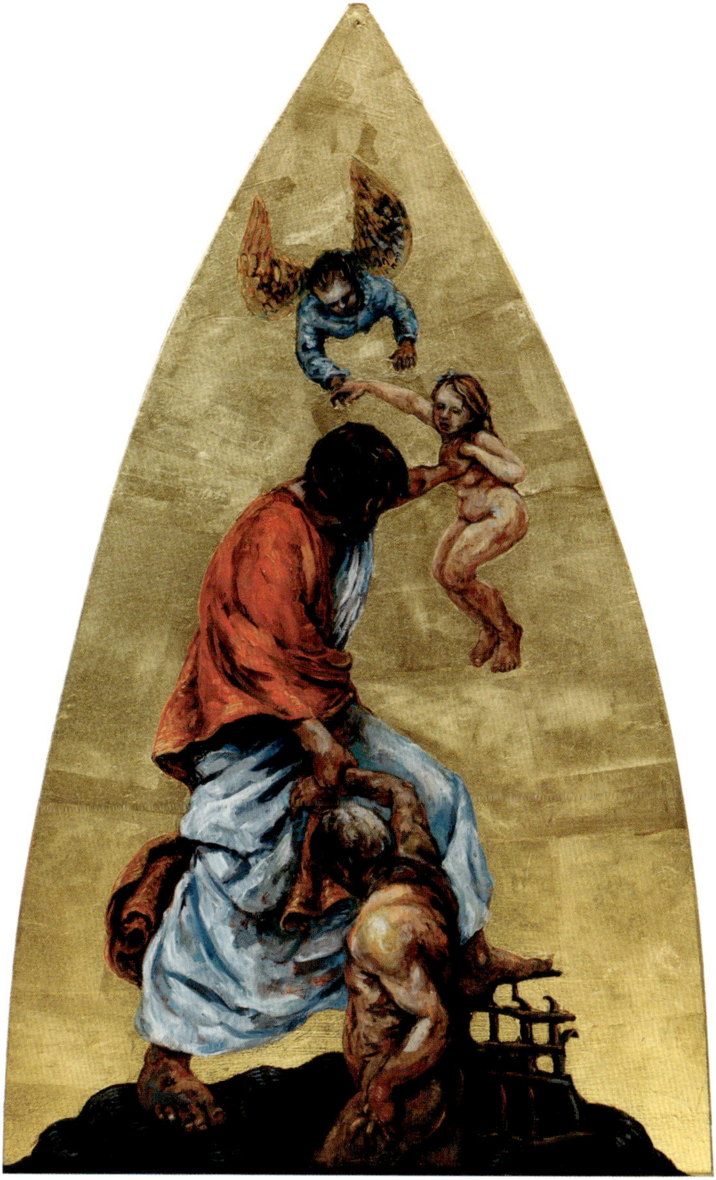

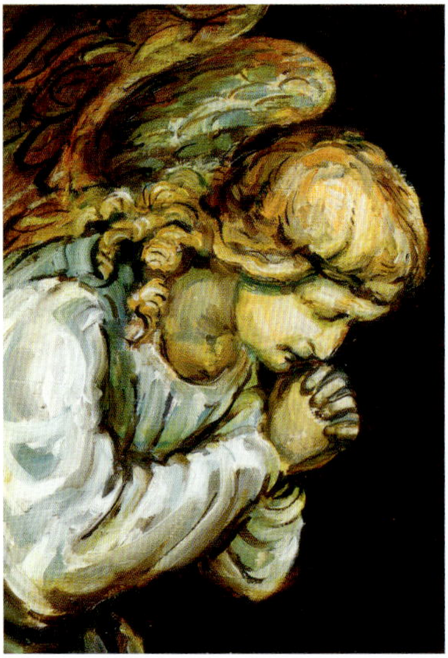

Love Bade Me Welcome

Love bade me welcome: yet my soul drew back.
Guiltie of dust and sinne.
But quick-ey'd Love, observing me grow slack
From my first entrance in,
Drew nearer to me, sweetly questioning
If I lack'd anything.
A guest, I answer'd, worthy to be here:
Love said, You shall be he.
I the unkinde, ungratefull ? Ah, my deare,
I cannot look on thee.
Love took my hand, and smiling did reply,
Who made the eyes but I?
Truth Lord, but I have marr'd them: let my shame
Go where it doth deserve.
And know you not, sayes Love, who bore the blame?
My deare, then I will serve.
You must sit down, sayes Love, and taste my meat:
So I did sit and eat.

George Herbert

Who gave you the ability to contemplate the beauty of the skies, the course of the sun, the round moon, the millions of stars, the harmony and rhythm that issue from the world as from the lyre, the return of the seasons, the alternation of the months , the demarcation of day and night, the fruits of the earth , the vastness of the air, the ceaseless motion of the waves, the sound of the wind ? Who gave you the rain, the soil to cultivate, food to eat, arts, houses, laws, a republic, cultivated manners, friendship with your fellows?

Gregory Nazianzen

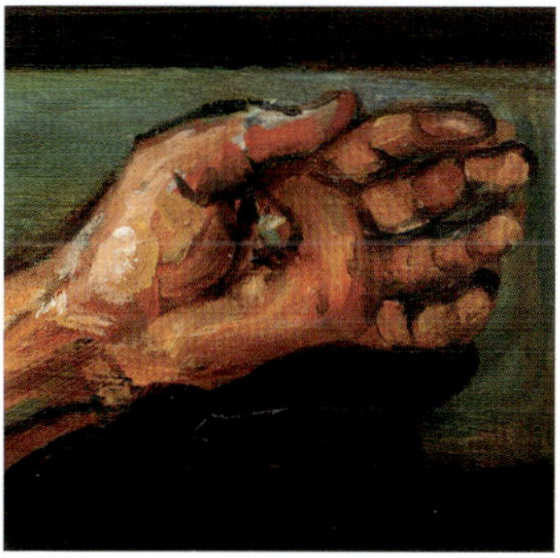

Stations of the Cross . Artists notes

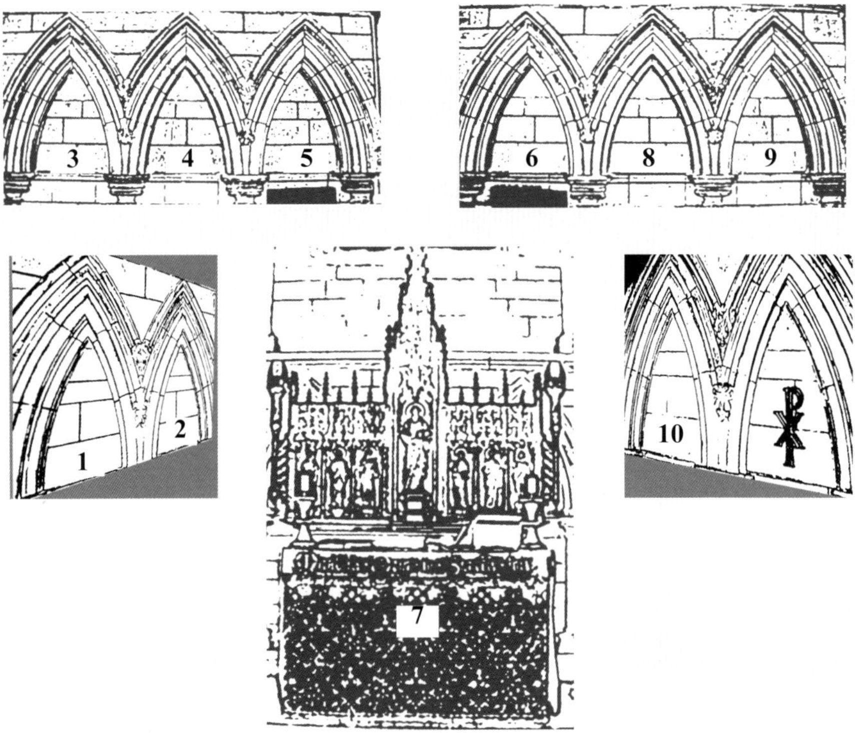

1. Jesus in the garden of Gethsemane - Jesus prays 3 times and is overwhelmed with what is to come. His three disciples have fallen asleep, (top right). An Angel comes to Jesus and carries a Finch, the symbol of sacrifice, death and resurrection. To the left, a lamb sleeps quietly, a red poppy beside him.

2. Jesus is Condemned - Pilate finds himself in an uncomfortable position . The crowd want blood, with the exception of one or two uncertain faces.The sky is beautiful and blue, with this cruel event happening below. Pilate's wife is seen to the top of the painting, she sends him a message, she has had a dream, he should have nothing to do with this innocent man.

3. The cross is laid upon Jesus - I found the torture and cruelty inflicted on Christ in the image of three Iraq boys playing war games, recorded by the media .

4. Jesus meets his Mother - Jesus remains Mary's baby.

5. Veronica wipes the face of Jesus - In my interpretation, Veronica going out out with the dog to pick daffodils finds herself on the way of the cross, and after wiping Jesus' face out of simple compassion, she shows us the cloth on which his image remains.

6. Jesus meets the women of Jerusalem - Here the women are together, but like standing stones, each lost in their own sadness.

7. The Crucifixion - I hung the two angels in space, to attend Christ on the cross, in a silent darkness. Their hands clasped in prayer at the suffering they witness. I did not want to include the crowds here, the light that shines on this terrible moment comes from Jesus' halo and from above.

8. Jesus is taken down from the cross - Christ is returned to those that love him. His Mother holds his lifeless body. Above Jesus' naked spirit rises towards God and angels who welcome him home.

9. Jesus in the tomb - His body is wrapped in linen, placed in a tomb carved into the rock, on Christ's chest are placed red carnations, a symbolic reference. In the composition his Mother and Mary are at the entrance, to accentuate the isolation and fear involved in death.

10. The Resurrection - A celebration, and a spectacle, Jesus returns and shows his mercy by descending into Hell, the folds of his clothing wrap around him, as he pulls a naked Adam and Eve from the darkness into the light, a winged angel guides them upwards, to heaven.

Artists Summary.

The ten oil paintings interpreting the Stations of the Cross were made over a two year period, specifically for the site in the All Saints Chapel. Nine of them fit into the Cathedrals stone arches, and at the front of the altar table is my depiction of Christ on the Cross.

The Stations began for me in the Garden of Gethsemane, where the terrible sequence of events lead to jesus being murdered, but conclude with the spectacle of his Resurrection. In my painting Christ pulls Adam and Eve from Hell having broken down the gates to release them, an angel guides them as they spiral towards heaven. Gold leaf holds the figures in space, a material used for centuries in religious iconography and imagery.

When looking at the paintings, we physically make our own journey from one station to the next. Some of my figures look out at you, inviting you in, to share their private moment, but with others, we bear witness to their grief and suffering. I wanted to reflect on the human side of those that take part in this story, they are caught in the moment. In these paintings I try to show people not confined to a distant past or place, but present, here in our own lives.

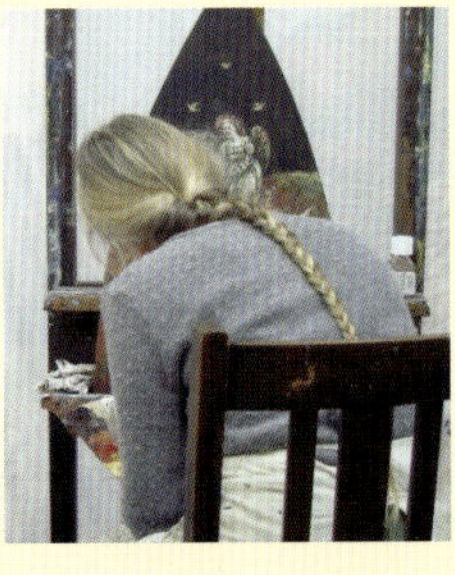

With special thanks to Very Revd Roger Bush, Dean of Truro, Revd Canon Philip Lambert, Carpenter Anthony Pascoe, photographer Steve Tanner and all the people that have helped me to make the paintings.

www.zoecameron.co.uk